CONFLICT REVOLUTION®
THE WORKBOOK

World Peace, One Person at a Time
Starting with You

Barbara With

Conflict REVOLUTION®
The Workbook

World Peace, One Person at a Time

Starting With You

© 2023 Synergy Alliance LLC
ISBN 979-8-9880337-2-1

For information, address
Synergy Alliance
P.O. Box 153
La Pointe, WI 54850
715.209.5471

www.synergyalliance.org

Book design: Barbara With
Inside Back Photo: Barbara With

Dedications

Dedicated to Teresa McMillian and Kimberly Lilith Phelps, without whom we could not have created this remarkable system.

To all the Conflict REVOLUTIONaries who contributed to the process, including but not limited to Tammera Logan, Barbara Daughter, Cathy Kline, Robin Cordova, Debbie Delung, Joanne Hunt, Steve and Carol Baer, Heike Zeitlmann, Ron Cerveny, Carmen Meera, Cristian Chitu, Nan Hedburg, Cassandra Schamber, Don and Donna Ross, Felicity Frazer, David Ransley, Holly Adams, Inga Holst, Jessica Sackett, Maria Kempe, Sherry Truenow, and the Crimson Circle, and Mary Laughlin.

To the always-inspiring Albert Einstein, whose wisdom guided the practical understanding of this practice of peace making.

And to all who have practiced Conflict REVOLUTION® around the world. May the peace be with you.

Commitment & Release

I, the undersigned, have read and understood the Mission, Goals, Objectives, Ground Rules, and Values required for participating in this Conflict REVOLUTION® Learning Experiment and agree to abide by those guidelines.

I fully intend, to the best of my ability, to apply these revolutionary steps to my own conflicts as a way to become the change, taking responsibility first and foremost for my own thoughts, feelings, senses, body, and every decision I make.

I understand that I do this of my own free will, and that I do not hold anyone else responsible for my decision to undertake this experiment. I understand that by working this process, this is not a guarantee, but instead an experiment in self-discovery, and I hereby release, waive, discharge and covenant not to sue and hold harmless from all liability, claims, costs and expenses whatsoever arising out of or related to any results of my participation in Conflict REVOLUTION®.

_____

signature

By moving forward with this curriculum, I have hereby agreed to this Commitment & Release

Table of Contents

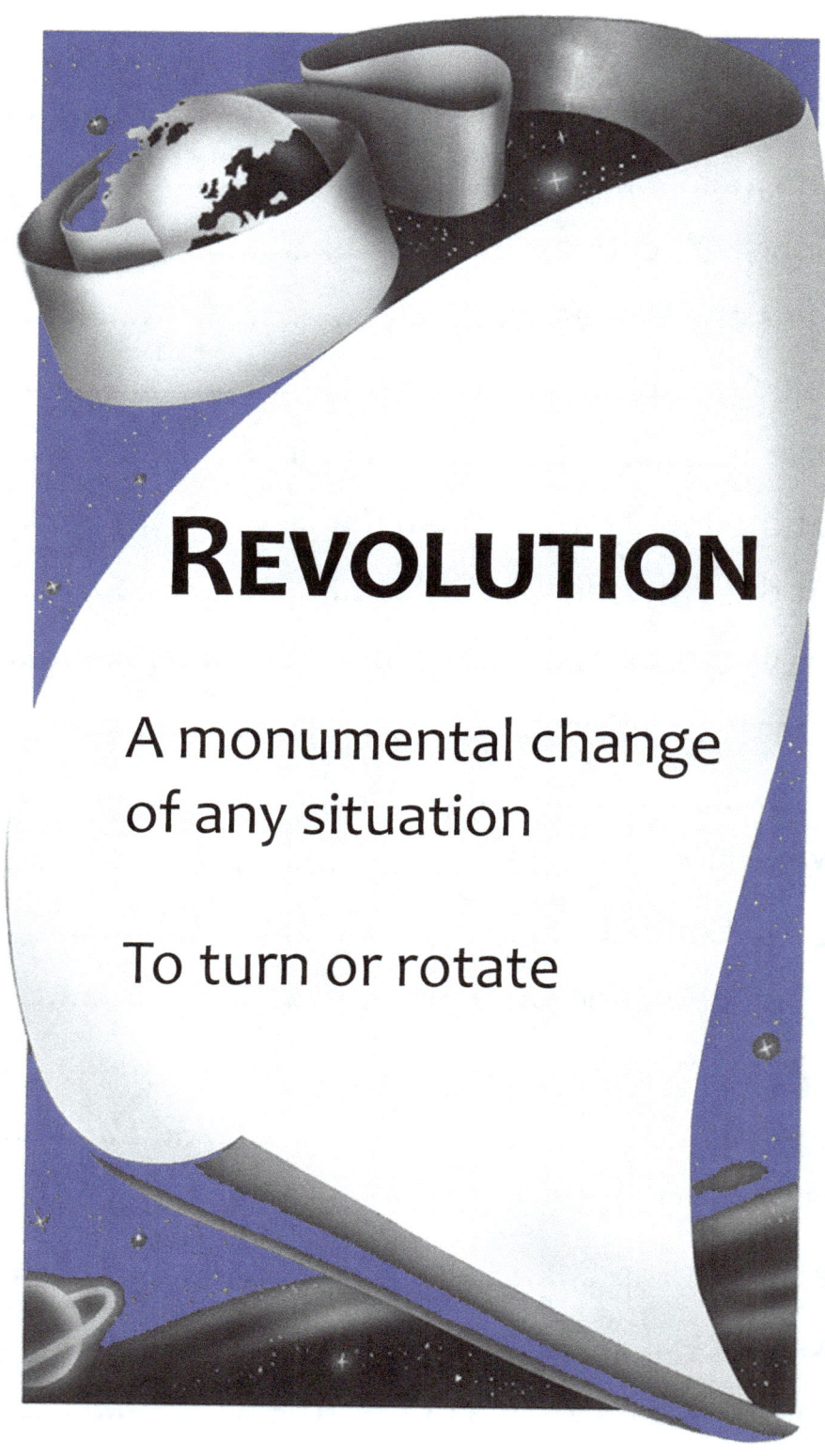

REVOLUTION

A monumental change
of any situation

To turn or rotate

CONFLICT REVOLUTION®

Conflict REVOLUTION®

Learning to Self-Love

Conflict REVOLUTION® is a revolutionary process to bring peace to your own energy field, called your *Domain*. Con REV® teaches you a new understanding of yourself and the roots of your conflicts, and gives you creative, effective, doable ways to resolve them at the root. By first resolving conflict within you, you greatly and naturally contribute to the resolution of conflicts going on around you.

When you learn to make conscious decisions "for the good of the whole" starting with yourself, you practice *self-love*, which allows you to thrive.

This is a journey of self-discovery and can be the hardest, yet most rewarding work you will ever do. After a while, though, as you begin to reap the benefits, making these healthier decisions becomes second nature. You will be Intuitively guided to take the baby steps needed to practice self-love on a daily basis.

Using this workbook, you will bring a conflict of your own and use the details to learn about your Domain and how to apply Con REV® to the situation. You will leave with an Action Plan and clear steps to inspire you to continue to make decisions from this place of self-love.

Learning to make decisions for the good of the whole will also contribute to world peace, one person at a time, starting with you.

THE BENEFITS

Happiness. More everyday moments are spent being happy instead of obsessed and conflicted.

Emotional well being. By practicing self-love in your daily life, you create a habit of managing your emotions in healthy and regenerative ways.

Independence. You are no longer dependent on others to resolve your conflicts. You can resolve them without the participation of the one you are in conflict with.

Better health. Once you learn to feel your emotions fully, deeply and richly you begin to experience better physical and mental health.

Increased energy and inner peace. Once you stop expending energy on emotionally draining and dead-end situations, you have more energy to spend on manifesting your needs and giving back to the world.

Fewer conflicts over time. As you bring peace to your inner world, so will your outer world be more peaceful.

More creativity. Once you start exercising your creativity in learning a new way to resolve conflicts, that creativity is available for other pursuits as well.

Taking action to influence peaceful outcomes. You no longer sit on the sidelines feeling like life is in control of you. You consciously and intentionally take actions to manifest peaceful outcomes to everyday conflicts.

Becoming a leader; inspiring others. By taking control of your own Domain, you become an inspiration to others and show them how it can be done.

Contributing to world peace. As you create peace within, you manifest peace in your local universe, doing your part to contribute to world peace as well.

CONFLICT REVOLUTION®

Mission, Goal, Objectives

Mission Statement

World peace, one person at a time, starting with you.

Goal

To learn a revolutionary new process to resolve conflict and use that process in everyday life.

Objectives

To identify, understand, and experience the components of your Domain—their form, function, and relationship to each other.

To learn to use Conflict REVOLUTION® on the details of a real-life conflict.

To develop a self-awareness of your Domain and change your own decisions in order to practice self-love.

To choose to use Conflict REVOLUTION® in everyday life.

GROUND RULES AND VALUES

GROUND RULES

1. *Your Domain is your responsibility*
You are here to focus on your Domain, not that of your neighbor, your father, or anyone else. *Your* Domain is your responsibility.

2. Your Domain is *your* responsibility
No one else can take care of your Domain for you. It is your responsibility to take care of it. Your Domain is *your* responsibility.

3. See 1 and 2.

VALUES

Passion
You not only have every right to feel all your feelings, it is your personal responsibility to feel all Emotion and make sure your feelings are flowing through you.

Creativity
Creativity is your birthright. We highly value using imagination to find creative solutions.

Nonjudgment
This is a science project. Objectivity is crucial.

Humor
Humor lightens the load.

 CONFLICT REVOLUTION®

YOUR SAMPLE CONFLICT

Pick a conflict, if possible, one that has not been resolved. Don't be too concerned with picking the "right" conflict. No matter which one you are drawn to examine, all roads will lead to the root of your part of the conflict. The drama of your conflict will help you understand your Domain, which is your responsibility to take care of and have dominion over.

Articulate your conflict. Write it out in detail: what stories is your mind telling you about this conflict? Who/what has triggered you? What have they done? How did it make you feel? If it's a situation and not a person, what predicament are you in? What judgments are you making about yourself and others involved? Who is judging you, and what are they saying?

You want to express exactly what your mind is telling you about the situation. Remember our values: be *passionate* and *creative* in writing about your conflict. Let yourself feel the feelings around it as you honestly and openly describe it. There are *no judgments* here, even of your judgments. In fact, we want to see your judgments so we can change them. This is where *humor* can help dispel the intensity of such deep self-scrutiny.

When you are done writing out your conflict, give your conflict a name. Part of naming the conflict is to inject some humor into what is normally a serious and confusing situation. "I am a Liar," "The Noisy Neighbors," and "The Drunken Marketing Manager" are some names that have been used to identify conflicts.

Sample Conflict

Below, briefly outline the details of your sample conflict:

_____
_____
_____
_____
_____
_____
_____
_____
_____
_____
_____
_____
_____
_____
_____
_____
_____
_____
_____
_____
_____
_____
_____
_____
_____
_____
_____

CONFLICT REVOLUTION®

YOUR DOMAIN

YOUR DOMAIN

Re-defining Who You Really Are

Your *Domain* is the totality of your life that you are in charge of. Everyone has their own and every day you have to deal with so many people's domains. It's important to recognize which domain you have control over and which you don't, and how to exercise that control.

Your Domain is much bigger than just your physical body. It is like having a house sitting on a plot of land made up of five parts:

✦ The Room of Intellect
✦ The Room of Emotion
✦ The Room of Intuition
✦ 1,000 Acres of Spirit
✦ The Witness

The old understanding of self has you thinking you live in a one-room house on a one-acre plot. Imagine discovering that you have three spacious and separate rooms and 1,000 acres that you never knew you had.

Understanding this new definition of self is the first step to creating your roadmap inward to your Domain.

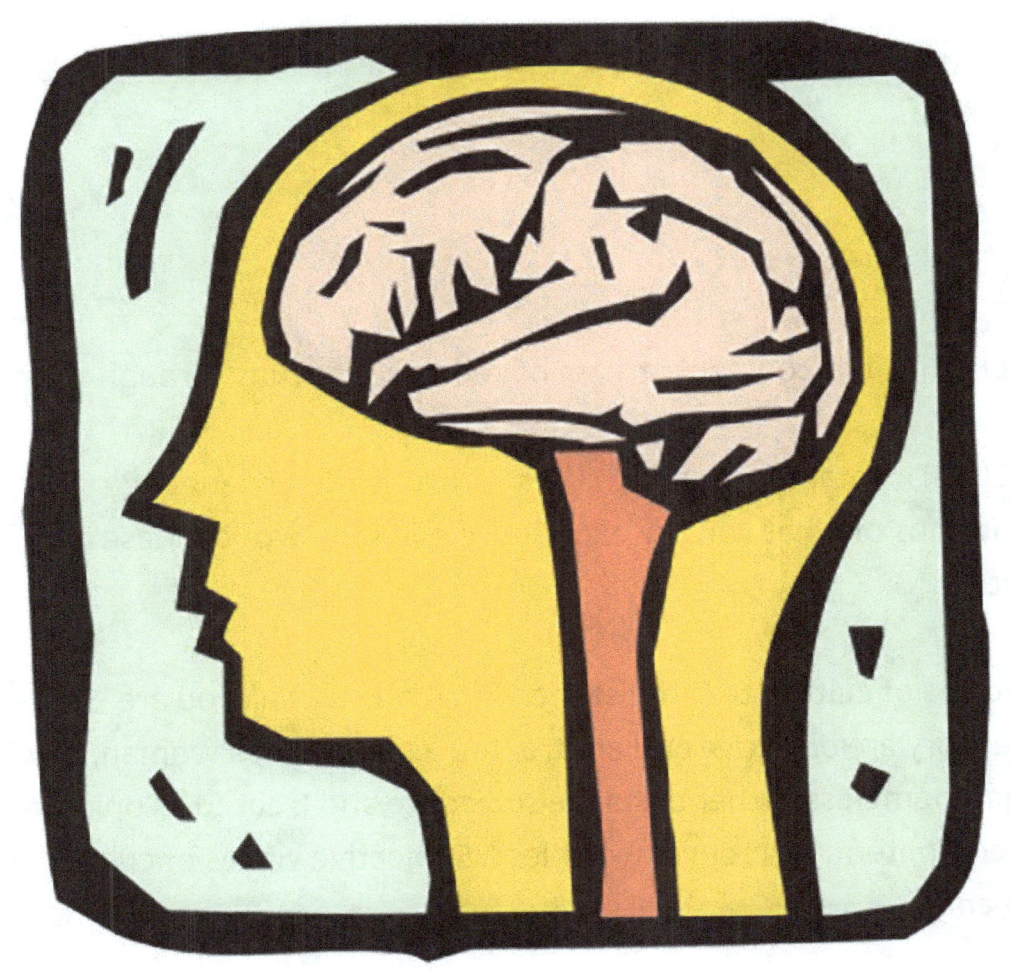

THE ROOM OF INTELLECT

The Room of Intellect

✦ INTELLECT is the constant stream of self-talk that runs through your head.

✦ INTELLECT contains ego, which uses imagination and language to create descriptions of what you are experiencing in your world. These are the *voices of culture.*

✦ The voices of culture tells the stories of who you *think* you are. Some parts of the story are *objective* and are treated as fact: I am a woman, black, a mother, homeless. Other parts are *subjective* and treated as opinions: I am ugly, competent, attractive, worthless. Subjective voices of culture are called *judgments.*

✦ INTELLECT will lie to you.

✦ INTELLECT is where all conscious and sub-conscious decisions are ultimately made.

✦ INTELLECT is home to Free Will and is located in the head.

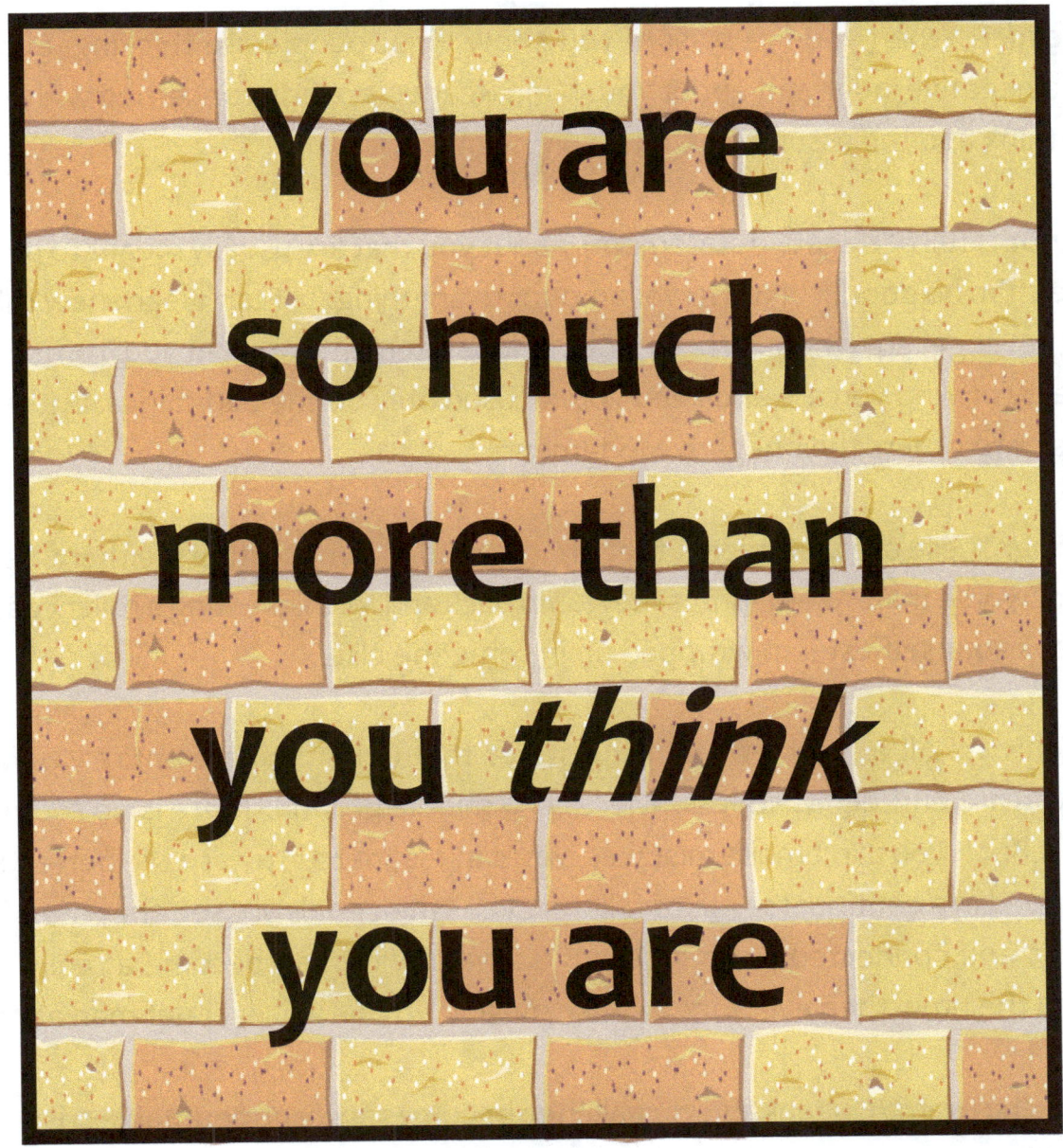

Negative Voices of Culture

Mind Reader: When you are so sure you know what people are thinking, and it's usually a negative judgment about you. Mind Reader is overly concerned with what people think and the assumption is usually negative.

Critic: Critic is full of negative statements about you that are usually meant to punish or judge. "I'm no good." "I will never amount to anything." "I can't learn new things and will never get anywhere." These judgmental statements prevent you from seeing the totality of who you are and keep you focused only on the bad things. Critic also projects onto others their negative judgments.

Comparing: These are statements that are comparing you to others, either "better than" or "worse than." Sometimes they jump back and forth, creating a roller coaster that keeps your self-esteem wrapped up in someone else.

Perfectionists: "All or nothing" thinking states that either you are entirely perfect or else you are entirely worthless. There is no middle ground. There is no room for mistakes. But if you can't make mistakes, you can't learn to grow, so the perfectionist is trapped in a continual sense of failure. Even when goals are set, they are often unrealistic and connected to an "if/then" scenario: "If I can become a really nice person all the time, then everyone will like me and no one will ever get mad at me."

Crisis Makers: Drama Queens. Every challenge becomes an insurmountable crisis that is bound to come to no good. Sometimes you create crisis for yourself because it's what you know and how you were raised. It's a chaotic comfort zone.

 CONFLICT REVOLUTION®

Affirmations

Affirmations: Firm and positive declarations

Intellect also produces the affirmations to counteract the negative voices of culture.

Transforming Low Self-Esteem

Identify some negative stories of the Intellect, and create new, affirming messages to replace them and redefine the situation.

Voices of Culture	Affirmations
I could never be a carpenter.	I can learn to be a good carpenter.
I will never learn.	I am in the middle of big change.
I won't succeed at this training	I am competent and can handle challenges
I am too weak.	I will work to get stronger.
I'm worthless.	I will learn to treat myself with self-love.
I screw up all the time.	I am learning from my mistakes.

Write some of your voices of culture and then create positive affirmations to redefine who you are.

Voices of Culture	Affirmations

THE ROOM
OF EMOTION

 CONFLICT REVOLUTION®

Feeling your emotions in present moment is not the same as *expressing* them.

Feeling is an activity using breath to move emotions through your body in present moment.

Expressing is an activity using Intellect to define, honor, and articulate what you are feeling in any given moment.

The Room of Emotion

✦ EMOTION is your passion; it is the essence of who you are.

✦ EMOTION is experienced as feelings flowing through your body that connect you to the present moment.

✦ EMOTION has no language or Intellect—no comparisons, descriptions, or judgments. There is only the pure experience of the raw emotion that you are feeling in any given moment: sadness, grief, joy, anger, happiness, frustration.

✦ EMOTION should not be repressed. Repressing your emotions takes away the mystery and chokes off the spontaneity of your life force, diminishing your ability to feel and is considered the root cause of many illnesses.

✦ EMOTION that is repressed doesn't just go away or vaporize. It get delegated to the Room in the Basement.

✦ EMOTION is located in the solar plexus.

 CONFLICT REVOLUTION®

The Room in the Basement

✦ A room that you may not even know you have, where all the feelings that you repress are stored.

✦ Repressed emotions can build up and eventually become overwhelming. They can then spilled out into your 1000 acres, into your Back Forty, that you also are unaware that you have.

✦ A build-up of repressed emotions in the Room in the Basement creates physical illness, lack of energy and motivation, depression and other mental illnesses, and contributes to all the conflicts you are experiencing.

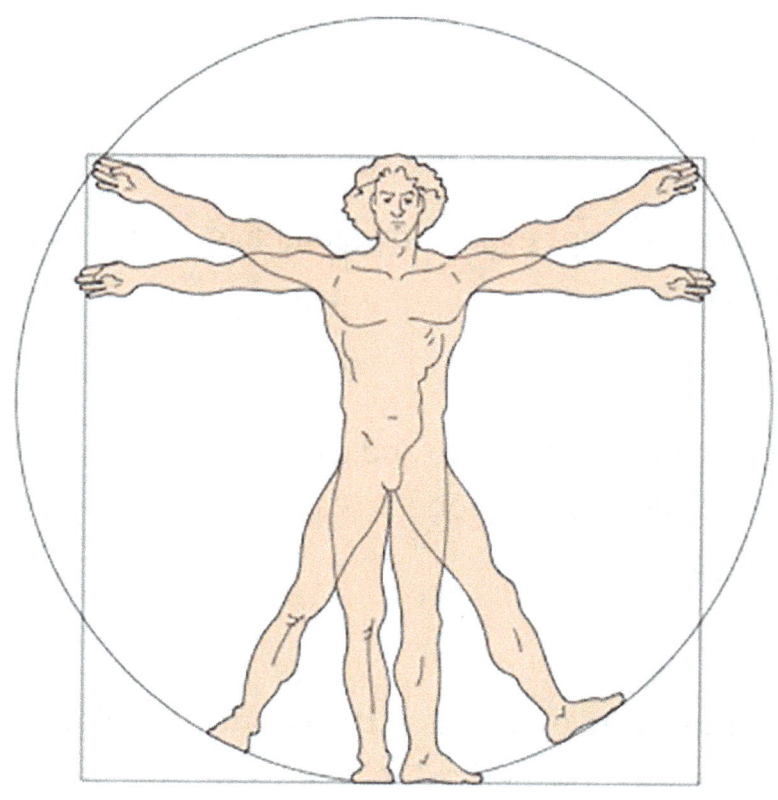

THE ROOM OF INTUITION

 CONFLICT REVOLUTION®

Intuition is the ability to know something without the use of rational processes

The Room of Intuition

✦ INTUITION is a small, imperative statement impelling you to take the next most advantageous step for the good of the whole. It is, in essence, the voice of self-love within you impelling you to take the next best step for the good of your entire Domain. It is a natural part of everyone's Domain.

✦ INTUITION is like having a room in the Attic with an antenna picking up signals from all across the 1,000 Acres. It knows what's going on in the entire Domain and is impelled do what is best for the whole of it.

✦ INTUITION can be experienced in several ways: as a subliminal message (the energy that is instructing your heart to beat without you thinking about it); as a physical feeling ("chicken skin," a gut feeling, etc.); as an unscripted action (stopping at a green light, only to have a car run the red light that would have hit you), or a language message relayed to Intellect ("Call your mom," Take the job," "Turn left").

✦ INTUITION is located in the heart.

 CONFLICT REVOLUTION®

1,000 Acres
of Spirit

1,000 Acres of Spirit

✦ 1,000 Acres of SPIRIT is the invisible life force that connects all the rooms of your house that all together make up your entire Domain.

✦ 1,000 Acres of SPIRIT is like fiber optical lines or wi-fi that carries Intuitive information throughout all parts of your Domain.

✦ 1,000 Acres of SPIRIT connects all the rooms of your house, but it's bigger than that.

✦ 1,000 Acres of SPIRIT is the boundary that separates your Domain from everyone else's Domain.

CONFLICT REVOLUTION®

Spirit is the vital principle or animating force within living beings

The Witness

✦ THE WITNESS operates within the Intellect and is an objective observer of your Domain who can consciously discern between your Intellect, Emotion, and Intuition.

✦ THE WITNESS, like the director of a play rather than the actor on the stage, can step back and analyze what's taking place within the Domain from a place of detachment and nonjudgment.

✦ THE WITNESS distinguishes between the stories in your head of who you *think* you are and who you *really* are based on observation of your own actions.

✦ Like a witness called to testify before a court who can influence the outcome of a trial, Witness attests to what is actually taking place in your Domain and possesses the power to influence free-will decisions.

CREATING YOUR LIFE

Every decision you make creates your life. Imagine how many decisions you make in one day. The more you can look at your life from the view of the Witness, the more you can *consciously* choose what decisions you make to respond to situations.

As the leader of your own life, you can learn how to make decisions that are in your own best interest. This is self-nurturing. As you nurture yourself, you make conscious choices about what you want and need based on what's best for you. In this way, you practice self-love, taking good care of yourself.

Remember, no matter what, you **always have a choice** as to how you will respond to life. By stepping back into your Witness, examining the situation, and choosing your next most advantageous step, you become the master of your own life.

What do you want to create?

How are you going to create it?

Notes

 CONFLICT REVOLUTION®

REVOLVING
THE CONFLICT

The condition of every

relationship

you have

is a

reflection

of your

relationship with yourself

     CONFLICT REVOLUTION®

Triggers, Projection and Detachment

Conflict REVOLUTION® is a process to discover your internal barriers: self-sabotage, low self-esteem, lack of confidence, and unseen conflicts. We will examine the relationship between your Intellect, Emotion, and Intuition, which will give us a picture of your relationship to yourself.

These three important tools have dual meaning:

Trigger: A person or event that appears to cause an emotional reaction (triggering event); the nature of the emotion itself: anger, hurt, offense, fear, etc. (triggering emotion). Becoming triggered—having an abrupt emotional reaction to a person or event—is the red flag signaling the need to adopt the reference frame of the Witness and prepare for a Revolution.

Projection: Defining the source of your thoughts, senses, or feelings as someone or something outside you ("he is making me mad"); **projecting judgments onto yourself or others** ("I am worthless"). Projection is telling yourself subjective, judgmental stories about something or someone outside of you, and/or about yourself.

Detachment: Letting go of projection; revolving your perception 180 degrees. As you detach from the idea that someone else is the cause of your feelings and revolve your focus back to yourself, you take control of your Domain. By redefining your world as originating within, you place dominion back in your free will. If you create it, you can uncreate it, and then recreate it.

THE ROAD MAP INWARD

From the perspective of your Witness, we are going to honor and articulate your sample conflict. Look over your Domain. The Trigger is actually a mirror for a condition that exists somewhere in your Domain that you're not aware of that needs your attention. This is an area of unexamined emotions, behaviors, and beliefs that have become barriers to your success.

In order to adopt the perspective of the Witness:

✦ Look over your rooms
✦ Listen to what is the Intellect saying (thoughts in your head)
✦ Pay attention to what Emotion you are feeling (feeling your solar plexus)
✦ Find the messages of your Intuition (message in your heart)

Let's begin to create your roadmap inward and an Action Plan.

Intellect

Referring back to your Sample Conflict, write down the top three reasons why you were triggered. Try to condense your reasons into two or three simple statements we will call "Intellectual Sound Bites" ("He doesn't respect my time"; "She's too needy"; "She can't forgive me."):

_____

_____

_____

_____

_____

_____

_____

_____

_____

_____

_____

_____

_____

Emotions

Referring back to your Sample Conflict, focus on how you *feel* about the conflict. Remember, feelings are simple and without explanation: anger, sadness, grief, loss, happiness, etc. How do you *feel* about this conflict? Refer to the list on page 40:

_____

_____

_____

_____

_____

_____

_____

_____

_____

_____

_____

_____

Intuition

Getting your thoughts and feelings out of the way, focus on what your Intuition might tell you is a step that you can make toward resolving your sample conflict. Remember, it's a small voice instructing you to take a step that would be good for the whole situation. This is sometimes difficult, but do your best to speculate (what would Jesus do? What would a spiritual adviser suggest?). Make sure it is an imperative statement that impels you to take an action ("Rest"; "Say you are sorry"; "Stay away from that person"):

_____

_____

_____

_____

_____

_____

_____

_____

_____

_____

_____

_____

Emotions

Absorbed	Carefree	Embittered
Adventurous	Cheerful	Enchanted
Affectionate	Cold	Encouraged
Afraid	Comfortable	Energetic
Aggravated	Complacent	Engrossed
Agitated	Composed	Enlivened
Alarmed	Concerned	Enthusiastic
Alert	Confident	Exasperated
Alive	Confused	Excited
Aloof	Contented	Exhausted
Amazed	Cool	Exhilarated
Amused	Cross	Expansive
Angry	Curious	Expectant
Anguished	Dazzled	Fascinated
Animated	Dejected	Fatigued
Annoyed	Delighted	Fearful
Anxious	Depressed	Forlorn
Apathetic	Despairing	Free
Appreciative	Despondent	Friendly
Apprehensive	Detached	Frustrated
Ardent	Disappointed	Fulfilled
Aroused	Discouraged	Furious
Ashamed	Disgusted	Glad
Astonished	Disheartened	Gleeful
Beat	Dismayed	Gloomy
Bewildered	Displeased	Glorious
Bitter	Disquieted	Glowing
Blah	Disturbed	Good-humored
Blissful	Downhearted	Grateful
Blue	Dull	Gratified
Bored	Eager	Guilty
Breathless	Ecstatic	Happy
Brokenhearted	Edgy	Harried
Buoyant	Elated	Heavy
Calm	Embarrassed	Helpful

 CONFLICT REVOLUTION®

Helpless	Moved	Spellbound
Hopeful	Nervous	Splendid
Horrible	Numb	Stimulated
Horrified	Optimistic	Surprised
Hostile	Overjoyed	Suspicious
Hot	Overwhelmed	Tender
Humdrum	Panicky	Tepid
Hurt	Peaceful	Terrified
Impatient	Perky	Thankful
Indifferent	Perplexed	Thrilled
Inquisitive	Pessimistic	Tired
Inspired	Pleasant	Touched
Intense	Pleased	Tranquil
Interested	Proud	Troubled
Intrigued	Puzzled	Trusting
Involved	Quiet	Uncomfortable
Irate	Radiant	Unconcerned
Irked	Rancorous	Uneasy
Irritated	Rapturous	Unglued
Jealous	Refreshed	Unhappy
Jittery	Relaxed	Unnerved
Joyful	Relieved	Unsteady
Jubilant	Reluctant	Upbeat
Lazy	Repelled	Upset
Leery	Resentful	Uptight
Lethargic	Restless	Vexed
Lonely	Sad	Warm
Loving	Satisfied	Weary
Mad	Scared	Wide awake
Mean	Secure	Withdrawn
Mellow	Sensitive	Woeful
Merry	Serene	Wonderful
Mirthful	Shakey	Worried
Miserable	Shocked	Wretched
Morose	Sleepy	Zestful
Mournful	Sorrowful	

Creating the Road Map

To create your Road Map, plug the information you have collected into a matrix, as illustrated below. Use the name of your conflict and identify the sound bites of your Intellect, Intuition, and Emotion. Organize them so that Intellect is at the top symbolizing your head, Intuition is in the middle representing your heart, and Emotion is at the bottom coinciding with your solar plexus.

Road Map

NAME your conflict:	
Intellect	
Intuition	
Emotion	

 CONFLICT REVOLUTION®

Sample Road Map

Here is a road map from a conflict that I had that I named "Bennie and the Maids." Bennie was a property owner who hired several maids to clean his rental properties. I was working for another rental property owner who made a deal with Bennie to share the maids with our company. Every time I went to pick then up, they were either not there, had already worked 40 hours that week, or Bennie would tell me I was wrong and they were not scheduled to work with us. At the time I had a bad back and shoulder. I kept telling my boss that I was in no condition to clean. But every time the maids were not available, I ended up having to do the turnovers. Here are my sound bites:

Road Map

Bennie and the Maids	
Intellect	Bennie and my boss have no respect for my physical limitations Bennie lies
Intuition	Make myself heard
Emotion	anger, sadness, rage, bitterness

Revolving the Conflict

Using the same creativity you called upon to create the sound bites, begin rewriting those Intellectual statements to revolve 180 degrees. If your sound bite is about someone else, make it about you. "He doesn't respect me" turns to "I don't respect myself" or "I don't respect him." Another form of revolving your sound bite would be by redefining a judgment into its opposite: "I am doing it all wrong" becomes "I am really doing this perfectly." "I am doing it perfectly" becomes "Maybe I am making a mistake somewhere." Use your creativity and imagination to find what resonates:

The Revolution

NAME:	
Intellect	
Intuition	
Emotion	

 CONFLICT REVOLUTION®

Revolving the Conflict

Revolving my Sound Bites was difficult. I suffered from the shoulder and back troubles for over a year. I had done everything possible to cure it: massage, acupuncture, physical therapy, rest, and nothing was helping me. Every time the maids did not clean, I complained to my boss about my physical condition, but he did nothing to help me. So seeing "I have no respect for my physical condition" triggered me into more anger, but I knew this was where I had to start to get to the systemic root of whatever this conflict was:

Road Map

Bennie and the Maids	
Intellect	I have no respect for my physical limitations I lie
Intuition	Make myself heard
Emotion	anger, sadness, rage, bitterness

Revolving the Conflict

By revolving your perspective back to yourself like this, you are putting control back where it belongs. The Revolution allows you to step into your Witness and to do a deep self-scrutiny of your own thoughts, feelings, senses, and ultimately the decisions that you yourself make.

Read your Revolution. Notice the emotion that arises when you consider that *you* could be the one who is not respecting yourself. Notice your thoughts when you realize that *you* might be the liar. Your ego's first and most natural inclination is to deny it: "No, it's not me, it's him!" or "I am not like that! I don't lie!" These denials and projections are part of the tricky ego trying to keep control, maneuvering so that you won't have to feel those repressed feelings listed on your Road Map or change *your* self-sabotaging decisions.

In truth, you have every right and responsibility to feel all of your feelings, and only you can take control of the wild horses of your Intellect. This is the root of your conflict and the imbalance Conflict REVOLUTION® is addressing.

Rest assured, this is not about letting people off the hook for their responsibilities. But going back to the ground rules—*your* Domain is your responsibility—you are not in charge of their Domain. Your Domain is *your* responsibility: this is *your* rage, not theirs, and only you can feel it. These are *your* thoughts and judgments. Only you can control and transform them. This is about you looking at yourself, and first and foremost, being 100% responsible for the decisions that you make in *your* Domain.

Learning how to love yourself requires two different skill sets, each one equally important, but serving two entirely different purposes. Instead of spending your time obsessing about the characters in your drama and worrying over its details, your job is now to learn these Conflict REVOLUTION® skills and inspire yourself not only to use them, but know which one to employ under which conditions.

 CONFLICT REVOLUTION®

Feel and Breathe

Feel and Breathe means experiencing Emotion as an energy and processing it using your breathing.

Feeling is not an intellectual analysis of what might have caused the triggering event. Yes, those details are needed to create Intellectual sound bytes. But analyzing the details of your conflict doesn't release the feelings that have been repressed for years in the Room in the Basement. In fact, thinking can *prevent* feeling by keeping you focused on the story in the Intellect. By focusing instead on breathing and affirmations that assist the breath to move those feelings through your body, you can change the way you process Emotion.

Emotion is your passion. You *want* to feel the full range of feelings—even the alleged "bad" ones of anger, fear, depression, etc. What you don't want to do is allow your feelings to automatically fuel thoughts of denial and projection. You use your breath and new affirmations to move all of your feelings through your body and free them at last from their prison in the Basement. By using affirmations to intentionally help your feelings flow through your body without judgment or attachment, you change the operating system, right before your eyes.

Feel and Breathe. Intentionally stop and take five deep, calming breaths. Use your Witness to feel Emotion in your solar plexus flowing up through your body, flowing out into the heavens through the top of your head. Detach from the story of why you think you feel this way, and replace those thoughts with affirmations that assist you in feeling and breathing.

By choosing to detach from the story of why you *think* you feel these emotions and actually taking time to feel them, you are practicing accountability and being a leader in your life. By doing that, you experience the intimacy and abundance of your present-moment. You are practicing self-love.

Affirmations for Feeling and Breathing

✦ This is not the time to think. Breathe!

✦ I do not need to know a story as to why I think I am feeling what I am feeling. I simply need to feel and breathe.

✦ Oommmmmm.

✦ Let go and just breathe.

✦

✦

✦

✦

✦

 CONFLICT REVOLUTION®

Revolving the Intellect

Revolving the Intellectual sound bites is a journey of self-discovery. Because your defensive ego is in the habit of projection, the Revolution can start a fight in your head. As you begin to hear the awakening truth and ego feels itself losing control, brace yourself for some internal backlash.

If your sound bite is, "He lies," its revolution becomes "I lie." Your ego's response to hearing this might be, "What? I am not a liar! I am one of the most honest people you will ever meet! Just ask anyone!" You might feel outraged at the suggestion that you are the one who is lying!

But this is not just about entertaining the idea that you are a liar. That is the first step. Then you must engage your Witness and commit to watch yourself throughout the day in order to catch yourself in the act of lying. The reason you create sound bites in the first place is so you can easily remember what you are looking for. Imagination can run wild and ego can create a cacophony of stories to distract you. The sound bite—"I am a liar"—cuts through all that and helps you focus on what you are intending to witness in yourself.

When you specifically watch for where you are doing the very thing that you are triggered by in someone else, you begin to change the operating system. You catch yourself in the act of perpetuating the very things that you are so outraged or hurt by in someone else. This self-witnessing is the most powerful tool for systemic change you can have.

Revolving the Intellect

The sound bite about lying is one most people can relate to. Your ego has a habit of continually lying to you with a steady stream of self-talk that diminishes your power and the miraculous truth of creation happening right before your eyes. The lies come in the form of subjective descriptions of yourself wherein you are a victim to yourself or others: you can't do the job well enough, you always screw up—it's your fault; or "they" always do this to you and "they" are the enemy—it's "their" fault.

Maybe you do not want to commit to spending time with someone. Intuition can be telling you, "Don't go," but the voices of culture say ... you can't disappoint the person, you owe it to someone, you can't appear disagreeable ... on and on come the lies that keep your Intellect in control. Instead of taking a step for the good of your whole Doman, you allow Intellect to override Intuition. You end up making a decision for the good of the ego at the expense of Intuition and Emotion. Identifying the lies and changing your thinking to listen to Intuition and implementing it will create the change.

Understanding and exercising this skill will revolutionize the way you interpret and respond to the conflicts in your life. You become more like the director of the play than the actor on the stage. As you commit to observing yourself, you focus more in present moment and less on the tape loop obsessively running inside your head projecting onto the actors in your drama. In doing so, you can choose to make different decisions, thereby facilitating different outcomes.

The act of feeling and breathing, observing your thoughts, and listening for Intuition gets you out of your ego and using the whole operating system. Intending to find the decisions that you yourself are making that are perpetuating the behaviors that you judge in someone else brings you to true transformation.

 CONFLICT REVOLUTION®

Action Plan

The goal of creating an Action Plan is to create a tool to help guide you to the steps that will resolve this conflict in your Domain for the good of all. You're watching for the very moment when *you* are making the decision to do the very thing you hate in someone else. Then, applying your new skill sets, you will be intuitively guided to the next most advantageous step to take for the good of the entire situation. At that point, you—and only you—will decide if you will take that step.

The moment you catch yourself acting out your intellectual sound bite is the very moment you empower yourself to make a new decision. Courageously facing the truth, you need to keep feeling and breathing while you listen for Intuition to reveal the next most advantageous baby step you can take into Self Love, right here, right now, to move the conflict into a resolution for the good of all. Then it's up to you to take that step.

The Action Plan

Bennie and the Maids	
Intellect	I will watch to see where I am not respecting my physical limitations and when I am lying to myself.
Intuition	I will listen to myself and make myself heard when I find myself making decisions that do not take into account my well being.
Emotion	I will feel and breathe all my emotions without allowing myself to attach to intellectual stories.

Action Plan

Bennie and the Maids

During my Revolution with Bennie and the Maids, I fought with myself internally. Clinging to the idea that I had done everything I could to heal my back and shoulder and it was Bennie and my boss who were the ones being disrespectful, I did not want to watch myself. But I persisted to step into my Witness despite the cacophony of thoughts the process was creating.

One day I went to pick up the maids. Bennie came out and once again told me that they were not scheduled to work that day. I had no choice but to drive out to the rental, which was a six-bedroom, three-story house that took six hours to clean alone.

As I was driving, I was raging! I watched myself ranting about Bennie and how he lied, and my boss and how he didn't care about me. In between the rants, I managed to also include my sound bites and began to ask myself where I am not respecting my physical limitations. With each thought, I raged some more, insisting that I had done everything I could. I went through the list of processes and activities I had done to heal my shoulder and back.

Stomping into the house, I began to clean. My Witness watched myself, both cleaning windows and raging at Bennie and my boss, while also asking where I was not respecting my own physical limitations. In one AHA moment, I watched myself use my bad shoulder to clean the window. In that moment, I not only observed myself not respecting my physical limitations, but how I was a liar! I had been telling my boss, "I do not clean," but each time the maids didn't show, what did I do? CLEAN!

In that one AHA moment, it all came clear. I sat down and cried. I asked my intuition what I should do: "Make yourself heard" came loud and clear.

Action Plan

I drove back into town and told my boss we needed to have a talk. I took him to the beach, sat him down and said, "I do not clean. I have been lying to you by saying that but then cleaning when Bennie's maids are not available. But that ends right now. From now on, I will not clean. You figure out how the rental will be cleaned, or when I get a call from the renters that the house is a mess, I am going to give them your cell phone number. I DO NOT CLEAN!"

My boss agreed to find a solution for the problem and we went back to the office. Literally a few minutes later, a woman named Betty walked into the office and said she had heard we needed cleaners and she was applying for the job. The issue was instantly resolved and I never had to deal with Bennie and the maids again.

After Betty was hired that summer, all my conflicts certainly did not disappear. But as I continued to use Con REV® to find the times I was lying and disregarding myself, I discovered many more situations where I was ignoring my own health, well-being, and happiness. Eventually, I revolved and resolved enough conflict to reach the fundamental questions: what is my wildest dream and what is getting in the way of making it come true?

When we revolve our conflicts and resolve them at the root like this, energy miraculously starts to work for us. When we resolve our inner conflict, that new congruent energy can manifest as creative solutions that we could not create ourselves. We had no idea Betty was available to work for us. It seemed like a "coincidence" but it was the result of working Conflict REVOLUTION®.

Revolving conflicts in this way will produce creative solutions you could not manifest going directly at the conflict in the arena in which it is playing out. Time and time again the resolutions that result are much more effective and lasting. That is the mystery and the miracle of Con REV®.

Action Plan

1. Before you get up in the morning, say a prayer of gratitude to be blessed with another day of life. Then pay attention!

2. Set an intention to be in Witness and observe your Intellect, Emotion, and Intuition as separate energies throughout your day.

3. Have patience with yourself while you are learning this new tool. Chances are, no one has ever taught you how to deal with conflict in a self-loving way or how to feel all your feelings.

4. Feel and breathe whatever Emotion is moving through you in present moment, without attaching it to a story. Remind yourself of your Emotional sound bites and create a new self-loving affirmation that supports processing Emotion by moving it through the body with breath while getting out of your head.

5. Carry your Intellectual sound bites around with you. Ask to be shown where you are perpetrating the conditions articulated in your sound bite. Pay attention throughout the day. Become a Witness and watch for when and where you are making or have made decisions that are creating these conditions.

6. Work to master the wild horses of your Intellect. Find ways to quiet the mind, such as yoga and meditation. Don't wait for a special time of day or a class to meditate; use the "unimportant" times, like when you are waiting in line at the supermarket or stuck in traffic, to cultivate your Witness, quiet the mind, and focus on the here and now. Do a quick 30-second scan from head to toe to settle down your thoughts. Step into your Witness and observe them with detachment.

Action Plan

6. When you have an AHA moment and catch yourself in the act of perpetuating your Intellectual sound bite, feel and breathe all triggering Emotion through your body. Use passion, nonjudgment, creativity, and humor to stay in the moment as the wave of Emotion passes.

7. Make a commitment to your Intuition. When you have an AHA moment, ask Intuition what the next most advantageous step is for the good of the whole situation. Then take it. Remember, it is a small step about what to do in that moment. In case of doubt, use this rule of thumb: if Intuition isn't emphatically indicating a step, do nothing for the moment, except to keep feeling and breathing.

8. Pay attention to what you are manifesting. Make a list of the small changes that are beginning to manifest. Notice times when you are less attached and can easily get out of your head. Be aware of the moments when you make yourself feel and breathe. Embrace the difficulty and discomfort of moving anger or anxiety through your body, but notice how much better you feel when the wave passes. Keep a journal and document the changes happening outside you. Pay attention to when a conflict "magically" resolves itself or when there is movement in an otherwise insurmountable block.

9. Celebrate the baby steps! Even though the changes might not resolve the entirety of the conflict, every step is part of the millions of baby steps you will take to do just that. Don't minimize the baby steps, celebrate them!

                    CONFLICT REVOLUTION®

Conflict Revolution Behaviors

Language

The language of Conflict REVOLUTION® will show up in discussions about conflicts. Use of the terminology as well as focus on the self as opposed to the other party of situation:

✦ "I was triggered..." instead of "s/he made me feel ..."

✦ "I was projecting" instead of "s/he was doing this to me ..."

✦ "My intellect was overbearing and judgmental ..." instead of "they were overbearing and judgmental ..."

✦ "I had to just breathe and feel"

✦ "My intuition told me ..."

✦ "I witnessed myself doing ..."

Focus

In a conflict, using Con REV will keep the focus on your own Domain, using only the other party's actions as part of the roadmap inward. Instead of blaming the other person and becoming preoccupied with the external circumstances of their actions, a Con Revver will talk about their part, their contributions, their Emotion/Intellect/ Intuition instead of the other party's actions.

Action Plan

A Con Revver will create an action plan for themselves based on the details of their conflict. They will be able to talk about the conflict and how it applies to their own action plan.

✦ "Mary really made me mad when she wasted my time, so I created an action plan to really be aware of when and how I tend to waste my own or other people's time."

Byproducts

Life becomes calmer, less chaotic. You can slow down, stop to smell the roses, get along better with people in general. Work loads become more manageable. Relationships become easier. Communication opens. Stress diminishes. Laughter is easier. For advanced practitioners, physical ailments abate, marriages are renovated, ex-husbands become allies, careers blossom, and families live in peace.

15-Minute Power Trip

Feel and Breathe
Five minutes while you focus on moving energy through your body using your breath.

Positive Affirmations
Five minutes
"I did the best I could and I forgive myself."
"I am a beautiful, wonderful, worthy human."
"I fully intend to let myself feel my feelings."
"I am grateful for ..."

Align with the Mission: Dream while you Feel and Breathe!
Five minutes
"I fully intend to create and become ..."

THE GIFTS OF CONFLICT

 ratitude
Thank the universe for bringing you another day of precious, mysterious, miraculous life. Revolving your conflict is an opportunity to get to know yourself and become the change.

 ntention
Intend to find your inner conflicts and revolve and resolve them.

 orgiveness
To forgive is to grant pardon without harboring resentment, and is for your own well-being.

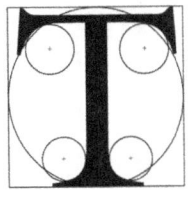 enacity
Have the tenacity to continue to revolve your focus and feel and breathe.

 elf-Love
The ultimate goal is to be self-responsible and self-regulating. This is the action of actively loving yourself.

Your life is your canvas. You are the artist. What are you going to choose to create?

CONFLICT REVOLUTION®

Making Your Wildest Dreams Come True

When you are practicing self-love in this way, Emotion flows freely through you, bringing with it the voice of Intuition telling you the next most advantageous step for the good of the whole. From the reference frame of the Witness, Intellect observes the details of what is being created in present moment, as well as listens for the Intuitive impelling. Then, like a faithful servant, Intellect uses free will to fulfill the Intuitive desire. If Intuition says, "Rest," Intellect immediately finds a way to rest—whether it's mind, body, or spirit. Intellect does not need to know why you are being asked to rest; it only needs to do it, in complete trust that Intuition is guiding the entire system to manifest an outcome for the greatest good for all.

The more you cultivate the Witness, the more control you have to use free will to make decisions aligned with your Intuition. The more you feel and breathe all Emotion, the more you are emptying out the Room in the Basement and releasing Emotion that has been repressed, perhaps for your entire life.

Imagine! What if everyone took responsibility for his or her own Domain? Energy that has been used in creating conflict would be freed up for intentionally creating peace and working for the good of all. People would tap into hidden talents they never knew they had. Everyone would be self-contained, self-loving, and self-monitoring; they would understand what they need and know how to fulfill those needs. Oh, how much different the world might be!

When you take full responsibility for your Domain and nurture yourself, you become a person of action instead of reaction, in charge of your own care and feeding.

Remember, no matter what, *you always have a free will choice* as to how you will respond to what is happening in present moment. By stepping back into the Witness and examining the situation, listening for the next most advantageous step and then taking it, you truly become the master of your own life.

Conflict REVOLUTION® is not about sitting on a mountaintop, away from all the cares of the world with nothing to do but meditate. Sustaining intimate, intricate self-awareness on a daily basis is one of the hardest things you can do, especially when you feel angry, frustrated, or threatened. The imbalance between Intellect and Emotion can have a tight grip on you. But persistence, hard work, and a strong commitment to your own transformation is what will change your life. Once you've changed on this root level, choosing self-love becomes knee-jerk.

Now when Emotion rises, an entirely new set of actions kick in, causing new reactions. Intellect knows to protect the world from its projections. It tunes into the messages of the Intuition and uses them to support feeling and breathing Emotion. You are a living truth, accepting your power, committed to and capable of contributing to world peace like never before.

If you want to be physically healthy, you create a routine of healthy eating and exercise. If you want to be spiritual, you routinely meditate and pray. If you want to be in politics, you routinely devote time to political causes. If you want to revolve your conflicts in this way, you take time to self-scrutinize on a daily basis.

If you can't get Intellect under control, step into your Witness and use your creativity to follow the clues to your own Road Map. Define what you think is the cause of your conflict, then set about to witness where you might be perpetuating these very conditions.

This kind of accountability and awareness is beyond science and religion. It is beyond politics and business, beyond humanitarian efforts. It is a transformation of the entire human species, one individual at a time, using free will to learn to love self. This is what will change the entire planet.

Notes

Notes

"Only one who devotes himself to a cause with his whole strength and soul can be a true master. For this reason, mastery demands all of a person."

"There are only two ways to live: you can live like nothing is a miracle, or you can live like everything is."

"Peace cannot be kept by force; it can only be achieved by understanding."

"To raise new questions, new possibilities, to regard old problems from a new angle requires creative imagination."

"I believe in intuition and inspiration. At times I feel certain I am right while not knowing the reason."

"Imagination is more important than knowledge. For knowledge is limited, whereas imagination embraces the entire world, stimulating progress, giving birth to evolution."

Albert Einstein

About the Author

Barbara With grew up in Minneapolis, Minnesota and currently resides in northern Wisconsin. She is an international peace activist, award-winning author and publisher, psychic channel, award-winning composer and performer, workshop facilitator and inspirational speaker.

Barbara has authored five books on metaphysics, including *Einstein, et al: Manifestation, Conflict REVOLUTION®, & The New Operating System* (2106), winner of the 2016 Best Book Awards for New Age, and finalist in the 2017 Book Excellence Awards for Body/Mind/Spirit; *Imagining Einstein: Essays on M-Theory, World Peace & The Science of Compassion* (2007), winner National Best Books 2007 Award for Fiction & Literature: New Age Fiction, and the 2007 Indie Excellence Book Award for New Age Fiction; *Party of Twelve: The Afterlife Interviews* (2001), winner of the 2008 Beach Book Awards for Spirituality; *Party of Twelve: Post 9/11* (2008), and *Diaries of a Psychic Sorority: Talking With The Angels* (1997, 2019) with Teresa McMillian and Kimberly Phelps, finalist in the 2019 Book Excellence Award for Spirituality.

Barbara has trained Con REV® since 1999 to thousands of people around the world.